LEVEL 1 SCIENCE

LET'S READ AND FIND OUT

THE SUN AND THE MOON.

BY CAROLYN CINAMI DeCRISTOFANO

ILLUSTRATED BY TAIA MORLEY

HARPER

An Imprint of HarperCollinsPublishers

Special thanks to Bradley J. Thomson, Ph.D., Senior Research Scientist at the Boston University Center for Remote Sensing, for his valuable assistance.

The Let's-Read-and-Find-Out Science book series was originated by Dr. Franklyn M. Branley, Astronomer Emeritus and former Chairman of the American Museum of Natural History-Hayden Planetarium, and was formerly co-edited by him and Dr. Roma Gans, Professor Emeritus of Childhood Education, Teachers College, Columbia University. Text and illustrations for each of the books in the series are checked for accuracy by an expert in the relevant field. For more information about Let's-Read-and-Find-Out Science books, write to HarperCollins Children's Books, 195 Broadway, New York, NY 10007, or visit our website at www.letsreadandfindout.com.

Library of Congress Cataloging-in-Publication Data
DeCristofano, Carolyn Cinami, author.
  The sun and the moon / by Carolyn Cinami DeCristofano ; illustrated by Taia Morley. — First edition.
    pages cm. — (Let's-read-and-find-out science. Level 1)
  Audience: Ages 4-8.
  Audience: K to grade 3.
  ISBN 978-0-06-233804-4 (hardcover) — ISBN 978-0-06-233803-7 (pbk.)
  1. Sun—Juvenile literature. 2. Moon—Juvenile literature. 3. Earth (Planet)—Juvenile literature. I. Morley, Taia, illustrator. II. Title.
  QB521.5.D43 2015   2015018465
  523—dc23   CIP
                                                                                AC

The artist used watercolor and traditional media with Adobe Photoshop to create the digital illustrations for this book.
Typography by Erica De Chavez
16 17 18 19 20 SCP 10 9 8 7 6 5 4 3 2 ❖ First Edition

To my writer's group, Barbara, Brian, Deanna, Delia, Jenny, Kim, Leslie, Mary, Wiesy, and Val. Thank you for helping me reach for the Moon.

—C.C.D.

For my parents, Frank and Val. Always there for us, day and night.

—T.M.

What's that round, yellow object shining in the sky?
    The Sun, of course!

And what's the other bright object up there?

Did you say the Moon? Then you were right. But sometimes the Moon is harder to recognize.

9

The Sun is out in the day. It always has a circle shape. But the Moon is different.

Phases of the Moon

The Moon seems to change shape. Each shape is a different Moon phase. Which of these phases have you seen?

New Moon

Waxing Crescent Moon

Full Moon

Waning Crescent Moon

New Moon

Sometimes you see the Moon in the daytime, sometimes at night. Its shape seems to change.

Wouldn't it be nice if we could visit and explore the Sun and the Moon? But they are so far away! Well, we can *imagine* that trip! Ready?

3... 2...1...

Blast off!
Away we go.

Up,
up,
up.

Past rooftops, clouds, airplanes.

12

Look! Down, down, down. There's Earth, fat and round. Wispy clouds whirl above blue oceans, white ice, and land—gold, green, and tan.

Can you find the spot where you live?
Maybe.
Linger awhile and watch.

See how Earth
turns like a top?

Day

Night

Different parts of
Earth turn toward the
Sun and then turn away.
The parts of Earth that
are lit by the Sun are
in daytime.

The parts of Earth
that are in the shadow
are in nighttime.

Night

Day

Day

Night

We could gaze forever—but
we're on a mission. Onward!

How far is the Moon?

You would have to line up 31 Earths side by side to fill the distance between Earth and the Moon.

TO THE MOON →

250,000 MILES

Hundreds of thousands of miles from home, we arrive at the ball-shaped Moon. It's smaller than Earth but the same shape, a **3-D sphere**, round in all directions.

Let's zoom to the daytime side of the Moon for a good look.

See those dark patches? Some people imagined that they were oceans, but **Moon seas** are rock. They formed long ago, when giant pools of **lava** cooled and hardened—think of gooey chocolate sauce freezing on ice cream.

Bumpy mountains and splotchy **craters** cover higher ground. What made them? Have you ever dropped a pebble into a puddle? *Plop! Splatter!* Water splashes out. Craters formed like splashes.

Billions of years ago . . .

Now...

Way back in time, huge and small space rocks crashed into the Moon. *Smash! Shatter!* Chunks and smithereens of broken Moon scattered. They left holes with high edges. Quick craters and instant mountains!

The Moon's craters, mountains, and seas have barely changed in billions of years. That's because the Moon's not like Earth. There's not much to move Moon dirt around. There's no flowing water, no air, wind, or weather.

Pssst. Some of these old, unchanging craters hide an ancient secret:

Ice!

Scientists think this frozen water is mixed with Moon dirt—like dirty snow. There's no skating here!

MAKE MOON ICE

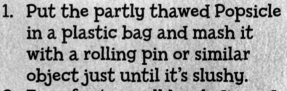

Gather:

- Popsicle (not for snacking!)
- Plastic bag
- Rolling pin
- Small bowl
- Small handful of sand

1. Put the partly thawed Popsicle in a plastic bag and mash it with a rolling pin or similar object just until it's slushy.
2. Transfer to small bowl; discard Popsicle stick.
3. Mix in 1 or 2 spoonfuls of sand.
4. Place in freezer and allow to refreeze (about 1 hour).

Take a look! You have something like the dirty **lunar** ice trapped in the craters that are on the coldest parts of the Moon.

There's something else familiar on the Moon: stuff from Earth.

There are robots sent recently by curious scientists.

A space exploration robot.

And there's older stuff, too. About fifty years ago, astronauts visited the Moon. They left some things behind . . .

Moon buggies.

Footprints!

Even two golf balls. (Astronaut Alan Shepard had fun hitting them!)

People marveled at these lunar visits. After all, for thousands of years, people looked up at the Moon. Finally, someone looked back.

Hello, Moon!

Hello, Earth!

And, now: *Good-bye, Moon.*
Here we come, Sun!

Astronauts have
been to the Moon,
but nobody has ever
visited the Sun. Can
you guess why?

The Sun is *much* farther from Earth—a three-*year* trip instead of three *days* to the Moon at your rocket's speed.

We're partway there, and look! Now you can see that the Sun is a sphere, like Earth and the Moon. But this is about all that's similar. You'll see differences as you get closer.

Stepping Out

1. In a safe, big space, mark a spot on the ground to be Earth.
2. Take one giant step. Mark this spot for the Moon's distance from Earth.
3. Take 388 *more* giant steps to show the distance to the Sun.

SUN

MOON

EARTH

For example, the Sun is *humongous*—you could pack approximately 960,000 Earths inside of it!

Want to land?

Sizing Up

The Sun is enormous compared to the Moon. Why does it seem Moon-sized from Earth?

Hold a penny-Moon in one hand, a Sun-quarter in the other.

Stretch out your arms.

Wink and move the penny closer to your eye the way the Moon is closer to Earth. See how its size almost matches the quarter's?

We can't. This blazing ball has
no land to land on.
    That's because the Sun is a star,
like the stars you see at night,
only much,
                much,
                        much closer.
That's why it looks so much
bigger and a *lot* brighter than
other stars, even from Earth.

Like any star, the Sun
shines on its own. It is
made of glowing, swirling
gases, similar to fire.
Imagine countless campfires
combined, with flickering
flames and flying sparks.

Remember how the Moon pretty
much stays the same all the time?
The Sun is so different. Just look at
all the action!

Sunspots skitter across the Sun. Think of these dark dots as great big wild **energy** storms that last for weeks. How big? A single sunspot is about the size of the *entire* Earth.

Here's a huge explosion, a **solar flare**. Every explosion sends bits of the Sun zooming into space.

Look at these giant, long loops of Sun material. Their name is almost as long as they are. Ready? **Solar prominences** (**prom**-uh-nun-ses).

There's also something you *cannot* see. It's the Sun's terrific heat. Parts of the Sun are *millions* of degrees hotter than a volcano or a rocket blast. So why doesn't Earth melt?

Earth does not melt because the Sun is so far away from it. That protects Earth from getting too hot. Luckily, though, the Sun is not *too* far away. It is close enough to keep Earth warm and for plants to have enough sunlight to make food.

The Sun helps us live. Think about it. Even from ninety-three million miles away, Earth is connected to the Sun.

You don't really need an imaginary trip to explore the Sun and the Moon. Just keep looking up.

Glossary

3-D (three-dimensional) sphere: A round object with a ball shape, different from a *flat* round object such as a plate. Having length, width, and height.

Crater: A hole made when a space rock crashes into a planet or a moon.

Energy: What it takes to make things move, heat up, light up, make noise, or change in any way.

Gas: A form of material that is not solid (like rock) or liquid (like water). A flame is a glowing gas.

Lava: Hot molten rock that comes from a volcano or from a crack in the surface of a planet or moon.

Lunar: Having to do with the Moon. Lunar ice is ice on the Moon.

Moon sea: A flat, dark area of the Moon. From Earth, it looks a bit like an ocean or sea.

Solar: Having to do with the Sun.

Solar flare: An explosion on the Sun that sends material into space.

Solar prominence (prom-uh-nunce): A giant loop of Sun material that stretches out from the edge of the Sun.

Sunspot: A dark area on the Sun that moves across the Sun's face.

Terminator: The border between day and night on the Moon.

Find Out More

Be scientific! Use your own eyes and pictures from telescopes to find out more.

KEEP LOOKING UP

- Keep a Sun and Moon journal. Notice and find out as much as you can. Write and sketch it all in the journal—including what you find out from the rest of the activities on this page.
- If you can borrow binoculars, use them to look at the Moon (never the Sun!). Find seas, craters, starlike dirt rays from some craters, mountains, and the border between day and night (or "**terminator**").

FIND PATTERNS:

- See if you can find the Moon every few days or nights for a month. Draw the Moon in your journal. Color in circles to show the shape of the bright part, and write the date by each picture.
- Every few hours, look for the Sun. Notice where it is in the sky. Be careful! Do not look directly at the Sun! Draw or write what you see. Check again the next day and the next. Do you see any pattern?

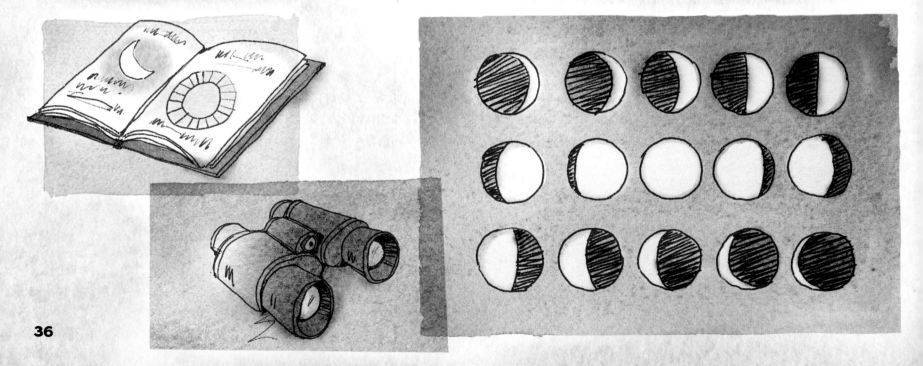

Read More and Visit Websites:

Learn more about the ideas in this book by reading these Level 2 Let's Read-and-Find Out books:

- *The Sun*
- *What Makes Day and Night*
- *Day Light, Night Light*
- *What the Moon Is Like*
- *The Moon Seems to Change*

SUN FOR KIDS:

www.nasa.gov/vision/universe/solarsystem/sun_for_kids_main.html

This book aligns with the Next Generation Science Standards.

This book meets the Common Core State Standards for Science and Technical Subjects. For Common Core resources for this title and others, please visit www.readcommoncore.com.

Be sure to look for all of these books in the Let's-Read-and-Find-Out Science series: